Is it wrong to be eradicated from within?
Not if the Lord is putting you back together again.

ERADICATED

21 Day Devotional

Finding freedom from the past.
Breaking chains of addiction and sin one link at a time.

By

Teresa Guerrero

(eradicated - to destroy completely; put an end to.)

Case ID: 1-15136288001

Scripture quotations are used as credited throughout the text.

ISBNs

Ebook: 978-1-972003-14-5

Paperback: 978-1-972003-15-2

Hardcover: 978-1-972003-16-9

Table of Contents

Dedication

To my wonderful, faithful husband, Jesse; Thank you for being my constant love and for protecting my soul. Your love is a treasure, and you have been an incredible provider for our family. Without your support, I could not be the mother I am today. It has been amazing to grow together in the Lord and to see the man of God you have become. Thank you for choosing me. The strength, courage, kindness, laughter, and stability you provide make you an excellent father and husband. We are so blessed to have you. I love you!

To my four amazing children; Trinity, Titus, Thaddeus, and Maya: You bring purpose and meaning to my life. My greatest desire growing up was always to be a mother, and you are my greatest joy. I am so proud of you and love you with all my heart. Each of you was born with a destiny and a purpose, and God has an amazing plan for your lives. Always seek the Lord in every decision, honor His Word, and never forget that you are, first and foremost, children of the Most High God. He loves you so much; never doubt it.

"But seek first the kingdom of God and His righteousness, and all these things will be added to you."

— Matthew 6:33

Acknowledgement

My deepest gratitude and acknowledgments for the completion of my book. I would first like to thank the pastor and worship leader who inspired the writing of this book. His powerful message, "Leaders vs. Needers," changed my life and deeply convicted me to be a good steward of the giftings and calling that God has so blessed me with. It compelled me to want to make a difference, and it truly feels like it gave my life new purpose and meaning.

I would also like to thank the individual whose beautiful prophetic writings not only inspired me but also encouraged me to pick up pen and paper and begin to write again. You know who you are. Special thanks to the friends and leadership who have prayed for me and spoken encouragement to me and over me throughout the years. Seen or unseen, you have truly made a difference.

I also want to extend my thanks to American Publishers. You have made this experience flow so easily and with excellence; it has truly been a pleasure working with you. Lastly, and most importantly, I thank the Holy Spirit, who laid out the blueprint for this book. Every detail was so clearly directed by His leading, including the title. He was with me through it all, reminding me that nothing in my life is wasted and that He turns every situation around for good when we trust in Him (Romans 8:28).

Thank you all for your support and inspiration.

Blessings,
Teresa Guerrero

DAY 1

"For I am convinced that neither death nor life, neither angels nor demons, neither the present nor the future, nor any powers, neither height nor depth, nor anything else in all of creation will be able to separate us from the love of God that is in Christ Jesus, our Lord."

Romans 8:38-39 NIV

Eradicated

Eradicate me from within.

Remove from me all my sin.
Rip away from my soul those temporary bandages that I have placed on my bleeding internal wounds.
As if any pleasure of this world can relieve the pain that I am in.

I cannot change the wrongs that have been done.
I can only allow you to expose the shattering for what it is.

Take your light and shine it bright.
I allow myself to be exposed, vulnerable, raw.
As we explore the caverns of my heart and soul together, we are uncovering the scars of sin.

As I walk through this journey of freedom with Jesus, He is walking right beside me.
He is holding my hand, and in His other hand is a flashlight.

He is talking with me and comforting me.
He doesn't shame me or scold me.
He loves me and shows me the reality of what is hidden.

You see, He knew the sin was there all along.
He saw the cover-up.
He knew what was behind the pain, yet He still chose to dwell with me.

How can that be?
A love so true, so beyond anything I can comprehend.

It is so vast, so deep.
Take comfort and be encouraged in this…
Behind the veil, there's a bridegroom waiting for you.

He has been patiently waiting.
Jesus is here, ready to eradicate your pain, your rejection, your trauma, all the betrayal, all the sin, all the shame, and every dark addiction that was used to mask the pain.
It's time to be healed.
He wants His bride, spotless, clean, and free again.

Jesus, let that purity and light live in me.

"For you were once darkness, but now you are light in the Lord. Live as children of light (for the fruit of the light consists in all goodness, righteousness, and truth) and find out what pleases the Lord. Have nothing to do with the fruitless deeds of darkness, but rather expose them. It is shameful even to mention what the disobedient do in secret. But everything exposed by the light becomes visible, and everything that is illuminated becomes a light. This is why it is said: 'Wake up, sleeper, rise from the dead, and Christ will shine on you.'

Ephesians 5:8-14 NIV

Prayer

Lord, it's time for me to come out of my slumber and wake up. Expose all the darkness within. I allow myself to be vulnerable with You. You see all that is hidden, all that is broken. Shine Your light within.

I repent for looking to other things or any other love to bring comfort and satisfaction while I was breaking. Forgive me for turning away from Your gaze, as if You were the one causing me pain.

I give You permission to do what needs to be done to make me whole again. Thank You, Jesus, for setting me free.

In Jesus' name. Amen

My Reflections

DAY 2

"Hope deferred makes the heart sick, but longing fulfilled is a tree of life."

Proverbs 13:12 NIV

Restoring Hope

For what is your tree of life?
Mine, a strong, tall trunk.
Thick, deep roots,
Roots that are so thirsty,
they long to drink from the rivers of living water.
A thirst so deep it's never truly satisfied,
but always longing for one more drink,
Begging for just one more.

My treetop is thick and dense, and my foliage is beautiful,
Color green… so deep,
Providing shelter from the heat.
My fruits are large and taste so sweet,
Giving healing to those who taste and eat.

Many years ago, my tree was not ready.
It takes much time to grow nice and steady.

As the wind rustles through my leaves,
together with the Spirit of the Lord, I give a gentle breeze.
The sun nourishes me as I grow in its grace.
I lean into the warmth of its love and embrace.
It's where I set my gaze.

Apart from the sun (Son), I would die, shrivel, and fade.
I must stay with my face turned towards the sun (Son) rays—
Rays of hope and rays of laughter for all of my days.

"I have told you these things so that you may have peace. In this world, you will have trouble, but take heart. I have overcome the world."

John 16:33 NIV

Prayer

Lord, I place all of my hope in You. I find comfort and encouragement in knowing You have overcome the world and all my enemies.

Lord, I give to You all my brokenness, disappointment, and delays. I choose to allow You to satisfy my soul. You provide everything I need to grow in the waiting. I know Your ways are better than mine, and You hold my times and destiny in Your hands. I trust You.

In Jesus' name. Amen

My Reflections

DAY 3

"Jesus takes bread, gives thanks, breaks it, and says, 'This is my body which is given for you. Do this in remembrance of me.' He does the same with the cup after supper, saying, 'This is the new covenant in my blood, which is poured out for you.'"

Luke 22:19-20 NIV

Forgiveness Granted

Forgiveness has the power to grant us love.
Love has the power to grant us forgiveness.
Love holds on when nothing else will.
Love says yes when the world says no.
Love says there is a way when circumstances say there is not.
Love will last through the games and all the trials of life.

Iron sharpening iron makes love golden, forged to a fine point.
A sword, a love to pierce my heart, and so I bleed.
Never the same after that deathly stab wound.
Eye for an eye, tooth for a tooth,
Oh, not so!

Can we see love differently when the tables are turned?
Rejected and wounded, beaten and bruised, hurting and lonely, betrayed by a friend.
Nothing lasts forever, but eternity and love.
Love stands to the end. Christ died and was made our sin.
Jesus made my love be true,

For I love Him and He loves you.
Death can never still this love.
Faithful, He will be till this love becomes you and me.

"Our Father, who art in heaven,
Hallowed be Thy name.
Thy kingdom come.
Thy will be done on earth as it is in heaven.
Give us this day our daily bread,
And forgive us our trespasses,
As we forgive those who trespass against us.
And lead us not into temptation,
But deliver us from evil.
For Thine is the kingdom, the power, the glory, forever and ever. Amen."

Matthew 6:9-13

Prayer

Lord, thank You for what You did for us on the cross, for how You loved me even then. We will not forget. I will not forget.

You took the sins of the whole world on Yourself. You suffered a cruel death. You bore all of mankind's sin even though You didn't deserve it. You did it because You loved me that much, and You could not bear the thought of being separated from me for all of eternity. You didn't have to do it. You gave Your life for mine.

Thank You for Your unwavering love for me. Your body was broken for my healing. Your blood was shed for my sins, for my deliverance. Help me to love and to forgive as You forgave us.

The ability to forgive is such a gift. It is what love does. I choose to surrender any hate or unforgiveness that I have held against others who have hurt me, including myself. Help me to walk out forgiveness, receive Your forgiveness, and release freedom as I bring heaven to earth.

In Your name, Jesus, I pray. Amen

My Reflections

DAY 4

"The angel of the Lord went up from Giligal to Bokim and said, 'I brought you out of Egypt and led you into the land. I swore to give it to your ancestors.' I said, 'I will never break my covenant with you, and you shall not make a covenant with this land, but shall break down the altars.' Yet you have disobeyed me. Why have you done this?"

Judges 2:1-2 NIV

Bokim – Weepers: Bokim serves to remind you of the importance of obeying God's commands and the dangers of compromising with the surrounding cultures.

Giligal – Rolling Away: from Egypt to the promised land.

Redemption

Caught away in my sin. Don't know where to begin.

How did I drift so far? How did I fail?
One glance at a time, one moment too long.
I looked at the sin and I didn't break away.
I knew right from wrong. I knew not to play.
But the world around you says it's okay.
Compromise will kill you, rot you to the core.
It sets up altars in your life where you bow down for more.
Sin is a pit; it drags you to dismay.
One drink, two drinks, three drinks, four.
Soon you'll find yourself lying on the floor,
Broken, defeated, shamed, and despaired.
Who can I call on? Who really cares?

I cried to the Lord, forgive me once again.
Into the arms of my Savior, my rescuer, my friend.
He forgives, He redeems, He makes you all new.

Be careful not to turn back. He has great plans for you.
You see, He's a jealous God.
He is jealous for you.
He will not allow worship to another.
You cannot have your cake and eat it too.

Every idol inside, every altar you have made,
Break it down now; the excitement soon will fade.
His finest sacrifice of blood was paid.
Redemption.

"Then Haman said to King Xerxes, 'There is a certain people dispersed among the peoples in all the provinces of your kingdom who keep themselves separate. Their customs are different from those of all other people, and they do not obey the king's laws; it is not in the king's best interest to tolerate them.'"

Esther 3:8 NIV

Prayer

Lord, I repent of every idol of sin that I have set up inside my heart. Show me what they are. Forgive me for every altar I have built and for every worldly pleasure or compromise I have placed upon it.

Help me to eradicate them one by one until nothing is left but my worship to You. Help me to be like Queen Esther and her people, who refused to bow down to the culture around them. They knew what Your Word said: You were to be their only God.

You are my only Redeemer, and You make all things new. I give my life to You—fresh, consecrated, and committed to You. Use me for Your glory, Lord.

In Jesus' holy name. Amen

My Reflections

DAY 5

"When tempted, no one should say, 'God is tempting me.' For God cannot be tempted by evil, nor does He tempt anyone; but each person is tempted when they are dragged away by their own evil desire and enticed. Then, after desire has conceived, it gives birth to sin; and sin, when it is full-grown, gives birth to death. Don't be deceived, my dear brothers and sisters. Every good and perfect gift is from above, coming down from the Father of the heavenly lights, who does not change like shifting shadows. He chose to give us birth through the word of truth, that we might be a kind of first fruits of all He created."

James 1:13-18 NIV

Bikkurim (Hebrew) means firstfruits, a type of sacrificial offering offered by ancient Israelites. In the agricultural season, the first grown fruits were brought to the temple and laid by the altar, and a special declaration was recited. (Wikipedia)

God's spiritual harvest

A promise of more to come

A foretaste of total redemption

A model of dedication

A living sacrifice

Sacrifice

Father of lights, You made the sun, the moon, the stars, just like You made me.
A life that was chosen, full of destiny.
The art of value fills my senses.
I breathe You in.
A greatness was bestowed upon me apart from sin.
Virtue is my crown from within.
A sacrificial love poured out.
You made me begin again.

No longer tempted by the world,
Nor what it has to offer.
My life laid down before Your crown,
Jesus' sacrifice and slaughter.

"Therefore, if anyone is in Christ, the new creation has come: The old has gone, the new is here!"

2 Corinthians 5:17 NIV

Prayer

Lord, thank You that You became the sacrificial Lamb. When You died on the cross, Your blood was poured out for me. You sacrificed Your life for our sin so we could be free.

I hand over to You every temptation in my life. It is not You; You do not tempt with evil, but You give us a way of escape. Help me to live a life worthy of the price You paid for me.

I want to be all that I was created to be, a first fruit for You.

In Jesus' name. Amen

My Reflections

DAY 6

"For you created my innermost being; you knit me together in my mother's womb. I praise you because I am fearfully and wonderfully made; your works are wonderful; I know that full well. My frame was not hidden from you when I was made in the secret place, when I was woven together in the depths of the earth. Your eyes saw my unformed body; all the days ordained for me were written in your book before one of them came to be. How precious to me are your thoughts, God! How vast is the sum of them! Were I to count them, they would outnumber the grains of sand— when I awake, I am still with you."

Psalms 139:13-18-NIV

Image

A vision of loveliness, staring into my-face
A mirror of deception what a disgrace
I thought I knew me and what the world said I was supposed to be
Screaming at me, lying to me, how can that be?
There is a way that seems right, but in the end leads to death (Proverbs 14:12)
Our Heavenly Father knows what is right for us
His plan is the best
He formed me and made me exactly the way he wanted me to be
My hair, my skin, my toes, my teeth
My eyes, my nose, and even my knees
He thought of it all, and he didn't make a mistake
You are a unique creation never meant to be fake
Love yourself!
Stop trying to be someone you were never created to be
He looked at you and said it was good you are so pleasing to me
Only one of you, unique as can be
From the top of your head to the soles of your feet
That's how he made you
It's time to be free

"Do not conform to the pattern of this world, but be transformed by the renewing of your mind. Then you will be able to test and approve what God's will is—his good, pleasing and perfect will."

Romans 12:2 NIV

Prayer

Lord, thank you for making me. Change the way I think about myself and help me not to see beauty with the world's eyes and image of what is acceptable. Help me to be comfortable in my own skin. You didn't make a mistake when you made me. Forgive me for any ways that I have harmed myself with wrong thinking or actions. Help me to see myself the way you see me and help me to really understand just how much I am loved. Just the way that I am.

In Jesus name, Amen

My Reflections

DAY 7

"Submit yourselves, then, to God. Resist the devil, and he will flee from you. Come near to God and he will come near to you. Wash your hands, you sinners, and purify your hearts, you double-minded."

James 4:7-8 NIV

Resistance

How can I stop this desire within?
It's drawing me.
It's pulling me toward sin, sin, sin.
I must resist so it will flee
The temptation feels so great
But I desperately want to be free
There is no turning back now;
I have taken my stand, you see
This flesh is so strong
It has been fed for so long
Given into all of its appetites
And all of its needs
My spirit is weak
My soul has been meek.
It's time to rise up
Spirit within, speak!
With every act of resistance
I will become stronger
With every overcome temptation
I will be bound no longer
I have a choice
I have a will
I will eat of His Word
And have my fill.
I can drink in His Spirit
His goodness will satisfy me
Until all of my fleshy desires are gone
Until I am finally free

"I can do all this through him who gives me strength."
Philippians 4:13 NIV

Prayer

Lord, some days are hard, but I know I can count on You. You are the exact strength that I need. Help me to remember that everything I truly want and need is found in You alone. Only You can satisfy the hunger of my soul.

Help me remember the weight of the shame and guilt that comes with sin—remind me why I never want to go back there again. I believe that each time I say "no" to temptation, it becomes easier to resist, until the day comes when these sins no longer have a hold on me.

Teach me to walk in the Spirit so that I will not fulfill the lusts of my flesh, even if I have to take it one hour, one minute, or one day at a time. Just as Your Word says, I can do all things through Christ who strengthens me.

In Jesus' name. Amen

My Reflections

DAY 8

"Therefore, if anyone is in Christ, the new creation has come: The old has gone, the new is here!"
2 Corinthians 5:17 NIV

Renewed creation

Let me strip away all of my sinfulness
as I lay here in this heavenly bliss
A new heart and spirit within me and a new name
My insides unraveled, never the same
The old life is finished
I'm radically spun
His love for me so passionate;
I'm totally undone
Reconciled to God
My life is hidden in him
Moving forward in grace;
washed and clean within
A fresh start awaits for me
Now I'm all brand new
A new path for me to walk on
Now with a heavenly view

"I will give you a new heart and put a new spirit within you; I will remove from you your heart of stone and give you a heart of flesh."
Ezekiel 36:26 NIV

"Create in me a clean heart, O God; and renew a right spirit within me."
Psalms 51:10 NIV

Prayer

Thank you God for renewing a right spirit in me. Thank you for removing my stoney heart in exchange for a new heart and tender spirit that is sensitive towards you.

You are forming me into what you want me to be. I was created for your glory. Thank you for leading me into the right paths and giving me your perspective.

My feet will follow where you lead.

In Jesus name. Amen

My Reflections

DAY 9

"God, you are my God, earnestly I seek you; I thirst for you, my whole being longs for you, in a dry and parched land where there is no water."

Psalms 63:1 NIV

Thirst

I'm thirsty for You, the living God.
Only You can satisfy my needs.
This longing I have inside me to drink,
The capacity I have to hold You is bigger than I think.

My well is deep.
Your love is vast.
My soul not satisfied
Until I have You at last.

I sit in this silence
While I'm breathing You in.
Sweet kisses from You,
May it never end.

I open up my mouth,
I learn to receive.
Rivers of living water
That are flowing into me.

My one true Lover,
There will never be another.
Prince of Peace,
King of kings.

I can have You up close,
I feel Your breath on my cheek,
Wrapped in humility,
Spirit so meek.

Some may not know that You love us like this,
For my sins are forgiven, thrown into the abyss.
There is nothing in between us now.
Your love is limitless.

Jesus answered, "Everyone who drinks of this water will be thirsty again, but whoever drinks of the water I give to them will never thirst. Indeed, the water I give them will become in them a spring of water welling up to eternal life."

John 4:13-14 NIV

Prayer

Lord, I want to always be thirsty for You. There is nothing that can satisfy the way that You can. Anything else is a counterfeit and leaves me empty.

You have made us to drink and drink deep. We need You. You made us this way. Help us to learn to drink only from the rivers of water and wine that You provide.

In Jesus' name. Amen

My Reflections

DAY 10

"As the deer pants for streams of water, so my soul pants for you, my God. My soul thirsts for God, for the living God. When can I go and meet with God?"

Psalms 42:1-2 NIV

Desperate

I always think about You, Lord
You are always on my mind
I always feel You drawing me
Closer all the time

I need You now more and more
It leaves me in a daze
It's Your touch, I can't get enough
Your affection I do crave

Surrendered to You now
Nothing else can satisfy
Desires of the flesh shall bow
No longer worthy to gratify

Draw me away
Into the deep.
Spending time in Your words
Are my promises to keep

You kiss me so softly
These moments so sweet
I treasure every second with You.
May I always be desperate to meet

"Let him kiss me with the kisses of his mouth, for your love is more delightful than wine."

Song of Songs 1:2 NIV

Prayer

Lord, it's in my desperation that I seek Your face. When things don't always go my way, or when disappointment comes knocking at my door, I have to remember that You have a plan for me.

It's not in hard times that I should ever turn back to anything else. God, I want to stay hungry and thirsty for You. I want to be desperate for You always, because it's in that desperation that I find You. It's in that place of hunger and thirst that I meet with my Savior.

You are always drawing me closer to You, pulling me deeper. Help me always stay sensitive to You and desirous of Your touch.

In Jesus' name. Amen

My Reflections

DAY 11

"But thanks be to God that, though you used to be slaves to sin, you have come to obey from your heart the pattern of teaching that has now claimed your allegiance. You have been set free from sin and have become slaves to righteousness."

Romans 6:17-18 NIV

Captured

Extravagant love has captured my heart
Bound in a twist
Your tether I cannot depart
Freedom I can't resist

I've tried so long to find true love
I thought it was a miss
I've searched and failed every single time
My ignorance was bliss

My heart does pound
Was lost, now found
Promises that have bound
My allegiance with a kiss

There's freedom in You
A greater grace still
I've come to know of acceptance
Of eternity—that's Your will

My life is now Yours
I'm now hidden in Christ
A slave for Your righteousness
I've been bought with a costly price

"Do you not know that your bodies are temples of the Holy Spirit, who is in you, whom you have received from God? You are not your own; you were bought at a price. Therefore, honor God with your bodies."
1 Corinthians 6:19-20 NIV

Prayer

Jesus, thank You for dying on the cross for me. You've bought me with Your blood that You shed on the cross. My life belongs to You, and I'm so grateful.

My appetites and desires for things of this world are changing every day. I want to live a life pleasing to You now as I seek Your presence. No longer am I a slave to sin, but unto Your righteousness.

Help me to walk out my new freedom.

In Jesus' name. Amen

My Reflections

DAY 12

"And when the day of Pentecost was fully come, they were all with one accord in one place. And suddenly there came a sound from heaven as of a rushing mighty wind, and it filled all the house where they were sitting. And there appeared unto them cloven tongues like as of fire, and it sat upon each of them. And they were all filled with the Holy Ghost, and began to speak with other tongues, as the Spirit gave them utterance."

Acts 2:1-4 KJV

The Infilling

With arms lifted high,
I'm yielded to You.
Waiting in the shadows,
Come, do what You do.

I'm stirring for more,
Can't You see?
Longing for the moment
You come and fill me.

I hear a shaking,
I feel a rattle,
A thundering, if You will.
A ball of light,
Shining bright,
Exploding as I'm filled.

Winds of power,
Tongues of fire,
Cascading with a blaze.
A fragrant myrrh of liquid love,
Transcending with His gaze.

I'm not alone,
Though He sits on His throne.
A great mystery to me still,
How can this be,
Dwelling inside of me?
A love that's so free.
Holy Spirit is the key.

"And be not drunk with wine, wherein is excess; but be filled with the Spirit; speaking to yourselves in psalms and hymns and spiritual songs, singing and making melody in your heart to the Lord;"

Ephesians 5:18-19 KJV

Prayer

Holy Spirit, I ask You to come now and fill me with Your presence. Let me too feel Your fire and speak in other tongues. I need Your leading and friendship inside of me. I can't do this life without You.

Fill me with all that You have for me. Make me drunk with Your love. Put a new song on my lips and a melody in my heart. I yield myself to You. I give You permission to come and fill me up.

In Jesus' name. Amen

My Reflections

DAY 13

"The Spirit and the bride say, 'Come!' And let the one who hears say, 'Come!' Let the one who is thirsty come; and let the one who wishes take the free gift of the water of life."

Revelation 22:17 NIV

The Bride's Cry

Holy Spirit, come and have Your way
Take complete control
Blow through me like a wind and touch my soul

Let Your flames of fire grow higher and higher
Burn in my heart Your passionate love
Through every storm of life, You are my rock
My safe haven of refuge

Your arms of love, they do surround me
Your wings of mercy, oh, how they cover me!
Up and away, like an eagle, I soar
With vision precise, my eyes fixed on You

With Your strength, I fly into the heavens above every obstacle of life
So great is Your faithfulness
It reaches the heavens
Glory and power
Wisdom and honor
To You, my God, be all the praise

My friend, my Lover, my Counselor, my God
Is there nothing You cannot do?
Embrace me, love me, dance with me across heaven's floor
Jesus, come quickly for me, my Lord!

Eternity awaits for You and me
A love like no other
So sweet and kind
My soul, it longs for Thee!

Fill my cup now; I want it to overflow
Joy and peace, Your fruits are so sweet
Patient and kind, Your love so divine
Ravish me, God, with Your goodness and love
Intertwine our hearts so we may be one

My strong pillar of strength,
I feel so safe when I'm with You
Oh, that all may know You the way that I do

"For your Maker is your husband—the Lord Almighty is His name—the Holy One of Israel is your Redeemer; He is called the God of all the earth."
Isaiah 54:5 NIV

Prayer

Lord, my destiny has always been and will always be a part of Your bride. You have made me to worship, and forever I will worship You. I am Your beloved. You hold my times and seasons in Your hands.

My desire is for eternity, to be with You forever. I always hear You calling me to come up higher. I want to be where You are. Keep me thirsty for Your love until we meet face to face.

In Jesus' name. Amen

My Reflections

DAY 14

"And we know that all things work together for good to them that love God, to them who are called according to his purpose."

Romans 8:28 KJV

Accepted

Fully accepted
Fully loved
Nothing is hidden on the inside
Nothing hidden from above

You cannot rob me of this treasure within
You cannot bind me with tethers of sin
My heart is made pure, washed in Your soap
My soul comes alive while it glistens with hope

There are some who will reject You
Attack Your integrity with lies
You were made to rise above them
Just walk away from their disparity and sighs

Like sifting of the sands
Like breaking of the seas
Relationships will come and go
But the love of my Father never leaves

He holds me, He knows me
He grows me as He needs
Forms me into His special masterpiece
Crafted as He pleased

Though some will not understand You
May misinterpret or discard You
It's okay, just turn away
You're accepted and loved by the Father

"The LORD hath appeared of old unto me, saying, Yea, I have loved thee with an everlasting love: therefore, with lovingkindness have I drawn thee."

Jeremiah 31:3 KJV

Prayer

Lord, thank You for Your unwavering love towards me. Sometimes decisions happen, things are said, intentions are misunderstood, and relationships sever, but Your faithfulness is unending. Your love is constant. You accept me when others don't.

You see the beginning, You see the end, and everything in between. I may not fit into someone else's mold of what they think I should be or do. That's okay because I was made with Your blueprint inside of me. You always make all things work together for my good. I trust the process.

In Jesus' name. Amen

My Reflections

DAY 15

"It is of the LORD's mercies that we are not consumed, because his compassions fail not. They are new every morning: Great is thy faithfulness."

Lamentations 3:22-23 KJV

Mercy

I'm falling apart
My leaves are all scattered
I'm shivering inside
I hear all the chatter

The voices are loud
They block my own view
Accusations and disappointments
The judgments pursue

Caught up in this whirlwind
My thoughts spinning for truth
Then silence touchdown
His mercy blew through

In the quiet, He speaks to me:
There's nothing you can do
To stop the love from flooding your heart
This gift I have, brand new

Every day you wake up
A freshness to perceive
It calls your name and needs no fame
Washes away all your shame

The enemy will always try to taunt
Try to get you to bend a knee
Don't lend an ear to that spirit of fear
I've come to set you free

Torture cannot control you
Entice you, or steal
This love that's been paid for
With my mercy and grace at your will

"Let us therefore come boldly unto the throne of grace, that we may obtain mercy, and find grace to help in time of need."

Hebrews 4:16 KJV

Prayer

Lord, where would I be without Your mercy and grace? We deserve punishment, but instead, because of Your loving kindness, we receive forgiveness.

Thank You that You are always faithful to calm every storm inside of me with Your soft words and gentle touch. You surround me with mercy. I draw strength from Your grace. Every day is a new beginning that I am so thankful for.

In Jesus' name. Amen

My Reflections

DAY 16

"And no one pours new wine into old wineskins. Otherwise, the new wine will burst the skins; the wine will run out and the wineskins will be ruined. And no one after drinking old wine wants the new, for they say, 'The old is better.'"

Luke 5:37, 39 NIV

The Crushing

Scattered along the beaten path
On the outside of my view
Is a trail of fallen clusters
Just waiting to be used

Beautiful and ripened
Left without a clue
Some fallen, some trampled on
Others badly bruised

How did they get here, I wondered?
Were they pruned and then refused?
Some churches had discarded them
While others just overlooked or used

Only some were selected
To manipulate for a happy muse
This was never the Vinedresser's intent
His vineyard has been abused

The thieves came in and ravished it with sin
Thus stealing the Master's fruit
The gleamers walked by and let out a cry:
Oh, the joy in the crushing tonight!

For those who have fallen and were left to bleed
Some were rejected, overlooked, and deceived
The Master still has great plans indeed
He is not done with you just yet

So let hope arise with no more sighs
Many miracles are now on the way
You are not forgotten
Just hidden for this day

The wedding feast is coming soon
And awakening to stay
The best was saved for last, my dear
Its sweeter than you think

This crushing is refreshing now

He serves the finest drink!

"And the master of the banquet tasted the water that had been turned into wine. He did not realize where it had come from, though the servants who had drawn the water knew. Then he called the bridegroom aside and said, 'Everyone brings out the choice wine first and then the cheaper wine after the guests have had too much to drink; but you have saved the best till now.'"

John 2:9-10

Prayer

Lord, You save the best for last. I can't control what someone says or thinks about me. Some may choose me while others do not. Beauty truly is in the eye of the beholder. I just know You turn every situation around. No one else can control my destiny because it was never in their hands—it's in Yours.

I release all those who have hurt me and rejected me and could not see the value in who You made me. Thank You that You have healed my heart and are restoring my hope. You have the greatest plans. There is beauty in the crushing.

In Jesus' name. Amen

My Reflections

DAY 17

"I am the true vine, and my Father is the gardener. He cuts off every branch in me that bears no fruit, while every branch that does bear fruit he prunes so that it will be even more fruitful."

John 15:1-2 NIV

The Pruning

Glitters of hope renewed
Rays of newness have shined
All but a brief second
Thus, it's now pruning time

I thought I was doing so well
Obeying everything I was told
And yet somehow I feel the pain now
Of something I must let go

The pruning is so true
His love and grace so new
Though it hurts me to the core
He has plans for so much more

The growth was sincere
With all of its blossoms
Now scattered on the ground
While the wind blows and tosses

Sometimes the Master prunes us
This process is tried and true
It helps us to grow back stronger
Our fruits get bigger, better, brand new

Our branches can get broken, crossed
Or just out of view
He has to cut the damage back
And disappointments accrued

He's making a way for a better day.
Stay close to His heart and never depart.
It's time to grow up and mature.

"Abide in me, and I in you. As the branch cannot bear fruit of itself, except it abide in the vine; so neither can ye, except ye abide in me. I am the vine, ye are the branches: He that abideth in me, and I in him, the same beareth much fruit: for apart from me ye can do nothing."

John 15:4-5 ASV

Prayer

Lord, You are so faithful. I love how You watch over my soul. You care about every detail of my life. You know just the right time to prune me.

Sometimes it can be painful, but I know You do this so I can bear much fruit for Your kingdom. Help me to always abide in You. Apart from Your love, my life is meaningless. You see the bigger picture, and it's always what is best for me.

In Jesus' name, I pray. Amen

My Reflections

DAY 18

"You prepare a table before me in the presence of my enemies. You anoint my head with oil; my cup overflows. Surely your goodness and love will follow me all the days of my life, and I will dwell in the house of the Lord forever."

Psalms 23:5-6 NIV

The Chasing

You pursue me
You call me by name
You know where to find me.
There's nowhere where I can run
There's nowhere I can hide
You seek me out and find me.
Your love, it draws me
Out of the shadows
Out of the depths
Into your inner chambers
Where there is no solitude or regret
An awakening of my heart
A realization of the truth
I am yours forever, Jesus.
My greatest prize is you
One in spirit
A cloak for two.
Wrapped in your loving swallows
A table set for me and you.
I am aware of your presence
It provokes me to dine
A meal that is so intoxicating
Where the honey is so divine.
My heart is filled with hope
As this race is set before me
He has made a new way
For the victory this day.

An eternity set in his love;
That's my greatest calling.

"But one thing I do: Forgetting what is behind and straining toward what is ahead, I press on toward the goal to win the prize for which God has called me heavenward in Christ Jesus."

Philippians 3:13-14 NIV

Prayer

Lord, my heart is overflowing today with thankfulness. You chase me down. You pull me to your heart. Thank you for all of the good plans you have for me.

The only thing that I need to do is let go of the past so that's what I am doing. I let go of everything that has held me back and I will run the race you have set before me.

My greatest joy is being in your presence. I love you.

In Jesus name I pray. Amen

My Reflections

DAY 19

"For I know the plans I have for you," declares the Lord, "plans to prosper you and not to harm you, plans to give you hope and a future. Then you will call on me and come and pray to me, and I will listen to you. You will seek me and find me when you seek me with all your heart."

Jeremiah 29:11-13 NIV

My Journey

This journey has been long
This journey has been tough
To get to where I'm going now
I know I cannot give up.
His grace is way too rich
His mercy is way too high
The thoughts he has for me are good
This truth I cannot deny.
His plans I know are great
I will get to the other side
To continue on this path that set
I will take each day with great stride
He chose me before the foundation of the earth
To walk along his side
He knows every direction my feet will step
The completion of my destiny will arise
A blueprint of where I'm headed
My ears are open to hear
He doesn't lead my feet to disappointment
Just stay close to him and draw near.
He will get you to the places you need to be
Don't give up hope
In this journey you must stay afloat
Yes, he has great plans for you indeed
Just always bend a knee
As you call upon his mercy
In his faithfulness you will see

That the master holds the key

"Being confident of this, that he who began a good work in you will carry it on to completion until the day of Christ Jesus."
Philippians 1:6 NIV

Prayer

Lord, sometimes we do get discouraged. Sometimes it takes so long. Many times we will question ourselves if it's even worth it. Help me to turn off the lure and lies of the enemy that wants me to give up and turn back.

You started something good in me and you never give up on me even when I have given up on myself. You always breathe upon me new hope.

The life you have for me is good and you want me to prosper. Your goodness will always carry me through to victory.

In Jesus name. Amen

My Reflections

DAY 20

"Come, my children, listen to me; I will teach you the fear of the Lord. Whoever of you loves life and desires to see many good days, keep your tongue from evil and your lips from telling lies. Turn from evil and do good; seek peace and pursue it."

Psalms 34:11-14 NIV

The Pursuit

As I sit and ponder all the works of men
I'm reminded of a cockiness that is driven from deep within
A bit of pride can turn aside and raise hell and sin
To my surprise, succumb to the lies
A breach that can destroy all friends

When we are wrong, do we try to shift blame
Or can we see ourselves for doing the same?
Is it wrong to be right or right to be wrong?
All of it is frivolous in the end and doesn't make you strong

A right to be wronged and a wrong can be right
What stirs the conflict?
What causes the fight?
The truth can be hidden in plain sight

To uncover your own sin, it takes great might
Salvation has come to the left and to the right
Start seeking the truth and truth will draw near
In pursuit of God's kingdom is where we must steer

Together in unity, we fight through dismay
We are stronger together
Let all pride go away
Swallow the rebuttal; it's really not worth the breath

Seek peace with soft answers
Lay all anger down to rest

"For whoever would love life and see good days must keep their tongue from evil and their lips from deceitful speech. They must turn from evil and do good; they must seek peace and pursue it."

1 Peter 3:10-11 NIV

Prayer

Lord, forgive me for the times that I haven't spoken with intentions of peace, but only to be right. Let my heart be done with pride and the need to always win. Help my perspective to always be in alignment with Your heart and Your words.

Let me always pursue peace. Help me to think before I speak. I want my words to be sweet and to release truth. May I be a carrier of Your peace and be able to diffuse hostility and faction.

In Jesus' name, Amen

My Reflections

DAY 21

"So if the Son sets you free, you will be free indeed."
John 8:36 NIV

Into Freedom

Out of the darkness and into the light
Those chains broken off me
My soul is in delight

Shackles could not hold me
Sin did not play fair
The price that Jesus paid for me
Nothing to compare

His love overwhelms me
I feel His touch with heat
The enemy thought he could choke me out
Silence me with defeat

God's plan and purpose never failed
He never let me go
His faithfulness will always be my anchor and rock to hold

Freedom is the coat I wear
My clothes are mercy and grace
My shoes touch down
They glide around
Led by prosperity and peace

This freedom walk is not just talk;
It fills my senses with ease
Receive the finished work that was done on the cross of Calvary:
Every drop of blood
Every broken bone
And that crown of thorns that dug deep

He died for you and me, you see
He came to set us free

"It is for freedom that Christ has set us free. Stand firm, then, and do not let yourselves be burdened again by a yoke of slavery."
Galatians 5:1 NIV

Prayer

Lord, it is only through You that we can truly be free. Thank You for this freedom You have given me. Help me now to walk out this freedom and live a life worthy of the calling and destiny You gave me.

Thank You for healing me. There is always hope and forgiveness along this walk, full of mercy and grace. Thank You for the gift of the Holy Spirit, who is always with me. I am never alone.

Thank You for the mind of Christ You have given me that keeps me sane. Thank You for Your blood, shed for me, and for giving me the keys to Your kingdom and power over every demon and enemy. Thank You for Your angels that keep me and protect me.

Help me to live my life now with no regrets.

I love You, Jesus. Amen

My Reflections

About The Author

Teresa Guerrero was born and raised in Dallas, Texas, and moved to Houston in 2003. She became a born-again believer in 1993, which changed the course of her life. She now resides just outside of Houston with her husband of over 20 years and their four children, where she has faithfully served in local churches in various ministry roles throughout the years.

She has a heart for worship and especially loves prophetic dance, revival culture, and working with children. It is her greatest desire for people to walk in their God-given destiny and purpose while teaching others about their new identity, freedom in Christ, and the love of Jesus.

www.ingramcontent.com/pod-product-compliance
Lightning Source LLC
LaVergne TN
LVHW050942080826
845145LV00004B/1368

* 9 7 8 1 9 7 2 0 0 3 1 5 2 *